Beyond Mediocrity

BEYOND
MEDIOCRITY!

Answering the call to greatness

A 31-DAY DEVOTIONAL

Designed to help you maximize your potential and fulfill your God-given destiny.

NEAL GRAHAM

Library of Congress Cataloging-in-Publication Data

ISBN # 979-8-9885429-0-2

©2023 Neal Graham

All rights reserved. Printed in the United States of America. No part of this publication may be reproduced, stored in a retrieval system, or transmitted in any form or by any means, electronic, mechanical, photocopying, recording, or otherwise, without the written permission of the publisher.

Publisher: Neal Graham LLC

Tamarac, FL 33321

Printed by: Amazon

Cover Design by: Brian Dockery

Interior design/formatting by: Robens Chery

Principle House Publishing

Contact/Booking
Nealgraham@icloud.com
IG: @pastornealgraham
Facebook: Neal Graham

DEDICATION

I'd like to dedicate this book to my tribe: My beautiful bride of 32 years, Judy Graham, and my two other heartbeats, my son and daughter, Jonathan and Jordan Alexis. Thank you so much for encouraging me to put down in writing principles that are time-tested in our personal lives and that have guided our family, as well as each of us as unique individuals with various life assignments and destinies that have been ordained by God. Thank you to my brothers who made this project a reality Brian Dockery, your creativity is amazing, and I am so grateful for your life. Pastor Robens Chery the release of your prophetic word you released that 'it's time to release the volumes that are within' was a catalyst to bringing this book to fruition. And to the lover of my soul, Lord, I answer the call to do my part in equipping the Capital " C" church to do the work of the ministry. Thank you for entrusting me with the revelation of your word.

TABLE OF CONTENTS

Introduction 6

Day 1: The Difference Of 24 Hours 9

Day 2: A Clear Image 12

Day 3: Overcoming Guilt And Condemnation...15

Day 4: Letting Go Of The Past 18

Day 5: Rerouting 21

Day 6: New Direction 24

Day 7: Law Abiding Citizens 27

Day 8: Controlling Thoughts 30

Day 9: Under The Influence ....…..............33

Day 10: Willing To Change ...…..…......…..36

Day 11: Supernatural Increase 39

Day 12: Satan's Top Ten Playlist...................42

Day 13: Am I Really Spiritually Mature?.... …..45

Day 14: The Commanded Blessing 48

Day 15: God Is That You? 51

Day 16: Supernatural Wisdom .... …...54

Day 17: A Complete Recovery 57

Day 18: The Privilege Of Generosity .... .60

Day 19: Seven Years Of Plenty 63

Day 20: Why Am I Facing This Challenge? 66

Day 21: Back-to-Back Blessings 69

Day 22: Enduring The Test Of Time 72

Day 23: Right On Schedule 75

Day 24: Completely Outdone........................78

Day 25: The Satisfied Life 81

Day 26: Your Benefits Package 84

Day 27: Freedom From Containment 87

Day 28: The Real Secret To Success 90

Day 29: The Most Important Relationships 93

Day 30: Putting Blame In Its Proper Place 96

Day 31: Willing to Leave The Status Quo ……..99

Introduction

Something tells me there's more to life than what I'm experiencing!

"For I know the plans I have for you," declares the Lord, "plans to prosper you and not to harm you, plans to give you hope and a future." – Jeremiah 29:11 (NIV)

Have you ever looked at your life and circumstances and said to yourself, "I know there has to be more than what I'm experiencing?" I refer to that as the *divine itch*.

You see, if you are reading or listening to this book, you were ordained by God to accomplish greatness, experience a level of fame and distinction, and impact the entire globe with the gifts and talents uniquely given to you by the Creator of the Universe. But all too often, because of our current situations and the lies we have accepted from the enemy of our souls, we settle for a second-rate life and fail to live out our dreams and fulfill our God-ordained destiny.

We all have experienced the gnawing feeling that there is something more out there. More for our business, marriage, family, physical body, financial well-being and spiritual life.

As you read or listen through this book, you will be equipped with proven strategies and divine secrets that will help you unlock the greatness on the inside and move to your next level! I will share testimonies of ordinary people like yourself whom I have had the privilege of coaching and imparting these very principles for more than 25 years. Today, many of them are currently accomplishing great things and living the life that at one time only seemed like a dream.

This book will serve as your MAP (Master Action Plan) to help you get to your next level and turn your dreams into reality.

Warning! If you are not willing to invest time, effort and discipline, put this book down until you are. "How will I know I'm ready?" you ask? Because you will be sick and tired of feeling sick and tired. In other words, you will experience what I refer to as *divine frustration,* which is necessary to propel yourself into your next level and new season. You are called to greatness, but you must be ready to embrace the call!

I have two wonderful children of young adult age – my son Jonathan, a graduate assistant for the Florida International University football team, and my beautiful daughter Jordan Alexis, a third-year law student. I also have the privilege of 32 years of marriage to my beautiful wife, Judy. As parents, we both know that the responsibility and resources we can release and entrust to them now could not have been released and entrusted to them while they were infants or adolescents. Likewise, there is a spiritual principle that says, and I paraphrase, "When you grow up and can handle more, you'll receive more."

"What I am saying is that as long as an heir is underage, he is no different from a slave, although he owns the whole estate. The heir is subject to guardians and trustees until the time set by his father."
– Galatians 4:1-2 (NIV)

Did you hear that? You can own the entire estate but live like a slave because you haven't grown up or matured! And the father is the one who determines our divine timing of enjoying the entire estate solely based upon our maturing. If you've ever had the joy of teaching your teenagers to drive, you will relate.

I experienced this over the years as I taught both of my children to drive. We spent hours practicing, starting and stopping, driving in forward and reverse, on long winding roads, in empty parking lots, filled parking lots, and heavily congested areas of traffic. All of which helped them grow and learn to drive until the day I determined they could safely operate the cars that I purchased for them. Now they both enjoy the freedom of driving their own car, having a level of independence, and no longer needing to carpool with friends or use public transportation. That came as a result of their maturing.

Although you are called to a great life – key relationships, a better marriage, expansion in your ministry or business, stronger finances, deeper spiritual life, better grades, and a healthier physical body – none of this will be accomplished until you mature and renew your mind. Get ready to go Beyond Mediocrity and embrace the excellent life God has for you.

Neal Graham, Pastor and Life Coach

"Destined to win."

Day 1

The Difference of 24 Hours

Today's insight: With God, everything can change in twenty-four hours.

Today's verse: 2 Kings 7:1-2 (NLT)

Elisha replied, "Listen to this message from the Lord! This is what the Lord says: By this time tomorrow in the markets of Samaria, six quarts of choice flour will cost only one piece of silver, and twelve quarts of barley grain will cost only one piece of silver." The officer assisting the king said to the man of God, "That couldn't happen even if the Lord opened the windows of heaven!" But Elisha replied, "You will see it happen with your own eyes, but you won't be able to eat any of it!"

If you're facing a situation or problem that seems like it will last forever, I have great news for you today. Everything can turn in your favor in twenty-four hours. For some, this can seem impossible, but with God all things are possible. In today's verse, we read the story of a very difficult time in Israel's history – a time so bad that there was no food to eat.

Women were actually eating their own children to survive. That's about as bad as it can get. Then, the word of the Lord came through the prophet saying there will be plenty and things will be cheap in twenty-four hours. Sure enough, through a series of divine interventions, there was an abundance of food for everyone, and things were inexpensive. The only person who didn't partake of this miracle of provision was the person who had refused to believe the day before that things could turn around so quickly. Let this encourage you. If you will believe the word of God spoken through his servants, in twenty-four hours everything can change! (2 Chronicles 20:20)

Prophecy: I prophesy that your turn around shall be sudden, for the Lord will hasten to perform it. (Jeremiah 1:12)

Today's affirmation: With my faith in God, things can be different in my life by this time tomorrow.

Prayer: Thank you, Lord, for your amazing ability to turn every situation around in my life by this time tomorrow, in Jesus' name.

Reflections

Day 2

A Clear Image!

Today's insight: My self-image and knowing how God sees me will determine whether I reach my destiny!

Today's verse: Judges 6:12 (KJV)

"And the angel of the Lord appeared unto him, and said unto him, The Lord is with thee, thou mighty man of valor."

Will I fulfill my purpose and reach my destiny?

You may have asked that question yourself a thousand times, especially when your current situation and circumstances are screaming everything that contradicts that reality. If you have, I have a major spiritual key to share in today's devotional that if received and applied will guarantee you fulfill your God-given destiny.

What's that key, you ask?

Believe what God says about you more than what the devil, your feelings, circumstances, or people's opinions may currently be saying to you.

Whether you believe it or accept it, you have an enemy that hates you and fears you reaching your God-ordained destiny. Why? Because when you do, it will testify of God's great love, power, plan and purpose to use you to accomplish great things and affect your generation for His glory! There are seeds of greatness placed by God in each of us, but it's only when we begin to see ourselves as God sees us and believe what He says about us that we begin to live out that greatness.

In today's passage, we see that Gideon, like many of us before this revelation, had a poor image of self and God, but through an angelic visitation, God began to change his mindset. Once he believed who God said he was and began to walk it out, Gideon began to defeat the enemies that enslaved and impoverished him and the Israelites for years. Maybe today you feel like Gideon and ask *If God is with me, then why is this happening to me? Where are the miracles and breakthroughs He promised?*

The answer is, He is there with you waiting for you to believe what He says about you instead of your feelings or current situations! His promises are yes and amen toward you. Once this is received in your heart by faith and not just your head, you will defeat your enemies and receive the rightful inheritance of all His promises to you.

Prophecy: I prophesy to you this day, that your eyes are open to see who you are in Christ and the fullness of your inheritance in Him. (Ephesians 1:17,18)

Today's affirmation: God is good, He loves me and only desires the best for me. I am fearfully and wonderfully made and will fulfill my destiny.

Prayer: Thank you, Lord, for keeping your hands upon me and helping me to fulfill every plan you have for me, in Jesus' name.

Reflections

Day 3

Overcoming Guilt and Condemnation

Today's insight: Your new life in Christ is one that's to be lived free from guilt and condemnation.

Today's verse: Romans 8:1-2 (NIV)

"Therefore, there is now no condemnation for those who are in Christ Jesus, because through Christ Jesus the law of the Spirit who gives life has set you free from the law of sin and death."

Have you ever made a mistake or missed the mark badly? We all have. The Bible says we have all sinned and come short of the glory, but the good news is the following verse: *"...all are being justified [declared free of the guilt of sin, made acceptable to God, and granted eternal life] as a gift by His [precious, undeserved] grace, through the redemption [the payment for our sin] which is [provided] in Christ Jesus."* The secret to you being free from guilt and condemnation is the blood of Jesus, that not only cleanses you from sin and makes you righteous, but also goes to the root of your sin and, in the eyes of God, causes it to be expunged – erased, removed completely, annulled, deleted, omitted, or eradicated! In other words, He makes it as though the offense never even happened. Sounds too good to be true, but it is!

The next time you miss the mark, don't live in condemnation, instead follow God's cure for sin: confess it to God and then graciously receive His forgiveness by faith. (I John 1:9)

Even though your feelings may try to tell you otherwise, boldly decree in the face of the enemy, "I am free forever from my sin! I am forgiven! God has forgotten it, so I choose to do the same."

"I, even I, am He that blots out and cancels your transgressions for my own sake and will not remember your sins." – Isaiah 43:25 (AMP)

Prophecy: I prophesy to you this day, that your days of guilt and condemnation are over, and you will live with the consciousness of righteousness (right standing with God) from this day forward.

Today's affirmation: I am free forever from the guilt of my past and live in the freedom purchased by the Blood of Jesus.

Prayer: Thank you, Lord, for helping me to live free from guilt and condemnation because of the cleansing power of the blood of Jesus.

Reflections

Day 4

Letting Go of the Past

Today's insight: I can't undo my past, but I can have a new future.

Today's verse: Philippians 3:13-14 (KJV)

"Brethren, I count not myself to have apprehended: but this one thing I do, forgetting those things which are behind, and reaching forth unto those things which are before, I press toward the mark for the prize of the high calling of God in Christ Jesus."

Have you ever thought, *I really wish I could go back and undo some things?*
The truth is, we all have. And in most cases, we are not able to. My wife uses the phrase: "You can't unscramble eggs," meaning you can't change the past. However, the good news is in spite of how good or bad our past was, God always has a new beginning for each of us. In God, there are always new territories to conquer and the ability to start over again. That's really great news for those who have believed the lie of the enemy that it's too late for a new beginning.

Be encouraged with today's devotion that your in-Christ status gives you a new beginning each day.

"Forget the former things; do not dwell on the past. See, I am doing a new thing! Now it springs up; do you not perceive it? I am making a way in the wilderness and streams in the wasteland." – Isaiah 43:18,19 (NIV)

The enemy loves to keep us focused on our past. Why? He knows that focusing on our past can leave us feeling depressed and hopeless. And, if left untreated, depression and hopelessness can keep us stuck and try to convince us that our life is over and not worth living. Maybe you have had those thoughts. If so, don't listen! It's a lying, deceptive enemy who would love nothing more than to steal the awesome future God has planned for you!

"For I know the plans I have for you," declares the Lord, "plans to prosper you and not to harm you, plans to give you hope and a future." – Jeremiah 29:11 (NIV)

Starting today, forget your past and receive God's invitation to get in on the bright future and big plans He has for you! Begin to dream again and watch God bring those dreams to life.

Prophecy: I prophesy to you today, that the chains of your past are broken and, starting now, you step into the new season and future God has for you!

Today's affirmation: My future is bright because my future is in God, and my path is growing brighter and brighter. The longer I live, the brighter I shine. (Proverbs 4:18 MSG)

Prayer: Thank you, Lord, that my past is behind me, and my bright future is ahead of me. The best is yet to come for me, in Jesus' name.

Reflections

Day 5

Rerouting

Today's insight: No matter how far you've gone off course, you can get back on!

Today's verse: Romans 11:29 (NIV)

"...for God's gifts and his call are irrevocable."

Have you ever traveled to a new destination using the navigation on your phone and you hear the computer voice giving instructions to return to the route? As a Christian, you have an indwelling navigation system – He's called the Holy Spirit.

"...for as many as are led by the Spirit of God, they are to be called the sons of God." – Romans 8:14

You see, without the leading of the Holy Spirit in our lives, it's easy to get off course, derailed or hung up in a place, circumstance, relationship, business or career path that is out of range and very far from our destiny! The good news is, no matter how far you seem to have gone off course, or missed it, you must know that God hasn't changed His mind about your destiny! I love the story of Caleb and Joshua in Numbers 14:30. They refused to be denied entry into the land God had promised them. Out of an estimated three million people, most of which had refused to believe God's promises and veered off course, these two knew that God had not changed His mind. The Bible says they had another spirit – what I believe to be the spirit of faith. No matter what lies the enemy has whispered or is screaming in your ear, know that God hasn't changed His mind about what He has promised you. Allow the Holy Spirit to reroute you today into your Promised Land!

Prophesy: I prophesy to you that today is the day you get back on course. Your divine destiny will be fulfilled and every spirit that has tried to derail your destiny is broken, in Jesus' name!

Today's affirmation: I am a child of God who hears and fully obeys the voice of God. I lean not to my own understanding, but I acknowledge the Holy Spirit, and He directs my path. (Proverbs 3:5-7)

Prayer: Thank you, Lord, for setting me back on course and ordering my steps, in Jesus' name.

Reflections

Day 6

New Direction

Today's insight: God is bringing me into new things, places and relationships that I never knew existed!

Today's verse: Joshua 3:3-4 (NIV)

"When you see the ark of the covenant of the Lord your God, and the Levitical priests carrying it, you are to move out from your positions and follow it. Then you will know which way to go since you have never been this way before."

Do you like trying new things? Maybe new hobbies, interests, eating at a new restaurant or traveling to a new city? Because of what I'm called to do in ministry and in the marketplace, I'm constantly traveling to new cities, staying in new hotels, meeting new people and trying new places to eat. I must admit that although I'm not crazy about flying commercial, I do enjoy experiencing new places and people.

One of my favorite things to do is shop for clothes for myself and my family – completely opposite of my wife, who dislikes malls and shopping. When things get old and routine, they can get boring and stale. This is why God loves for us to sing a new song, and why His promise says He will do a new thing in us! In this season, expect God to bring unusual and new things into your life, be it in the marketplace or your mission field. God loves new things and He's releasing the unusual in your life today!

Prophecy: I prophesy to you this day that the new things that are in God's plan for your life are being released in unusual ways!

Today's affirmation: Today is a new day and season for me. Everything that is attached to me is experiencing God's new season!

Prayer: Lord, I lean into the new things that you have prepared and are releasing into my life in this season. I believe my best days are ahead of me and not behind me, in Jesus' name.

Reflections

Day 7

Law-Abiding Citizens

Today's insight: As a believer, I can enjoy the benefits of dual citizenship!

Today's verse: Philippians 3:20 (NIV)

"But our citizenship is in heaven. And we eagerly await a Savior from there, the Lord Jesus Christ."

Law-abiding citizens – that term can have multiple meanings, especially in this day and age of lawlessness we live in! But today I would like to impart new revelation and insight. As believers in Christ, we are citizens not only of the land of our birth and nationality, but we are citizens of Heaven, even as we live on earth.

This gives us dual citizenship and the awesome benefit of experiencing what Moses penned in Deuteronomy 11, "Days of heaven upon the earth."

We are ambassadors of Heaven who live from the economy and government of heaven. We are not limited to our native physical place of birth! Once we are made aware of our rights because of our citizenship, we can appropriate and enjoy all that our home in eternity provides for us.

We have authority, dominion, joy, peace, freedom from the captivity of the enemy and the ability to affect nations for the head of our nation's government, the King of Kings, the great I AM that I AM! Read your Bill of

Rights – your Bible – and begin to enjoy the benefits of your true citizenship of heaven.

Prophecy: I prophesy that your rights as a citizen of Heaven are being revealed to you this day: success, prosperity, love, peace, joy, great relationships and divine favor! (Psalms 103)

Today's affirmation: Because I am in Christ, I'm enjoying the rights of dual citizenship, of heaven and earth!

Prayer: Lord, I thank you for the revelation of my new citizenship in the Kingdom of God that has granted me extraordinary benefits and privileges, in Jesus' name,

Reflections

Day 8

Controlling Thoughts

Today's insight: My life will follow my most definitive thoughts!

Today's verse: 2 Samuel 9:7-8 (NIV)

"Don't be afraid," David said to him, "for I will surely show you kindness for the sake of your father Jonathan. I will restore to you all the land that belonged to your grandfather Saul, and you will always eat at my table." Mephibosheth bowed down and said, "What is your servant, that you should notice a dead dog like me?"

"As a man thinks in his heart, so is he." – Proverbs 23:7

Have you paid attention to your thoughts lately? I know it may not be something you've given much attention to, but in today's devotion, I'd like to insist that you do. You see, your life will follow your most definitive thoughts. That means if you're discouraged, defeated, depressed, bound by habits or on top of the world and winning, it's because you have consciously or subconsciously thought yourself into that place and space. The enemy of your soul works overtime to inject negative thoughts into your mind, hoping that you will take the bait so he can fulfill his objective to destroy your life.

In today's passage, we are introduced to Mephibosheth, the son of Jonathan, the covenant friend of King David. After the death of King Saul and Jonathan, King David seeks out anyone in Jonathan's lineage so that he may show him kindness. When David finds Mephibosheth and invites him to the palace, Mephibosheth is convinced it's to do him harm, but it was just the opposite. It was an invitation to have everything restored to him that belonged to the previous dynasty, of which he was of direct lineage. He asked a question, "Why do you want to help a dead dog like me?"

He was convinced that he was worthless and did not deserve the kindness of King David. What Mephibosheth didn't realize was that David was in covenant with his father, Jonathan, which meant that everything that belonged to David belonged to Jonathan and everyone in his lineage. So, the invitation to eat at the King's table was his rightful inheritance!

How much of your rightful inheritance are you doing without because the enemy of your soul has convinced you that you are worthless and don't deserve any of the blessings and promises of God?

Do battle today according to 2 Corinthians 10:4-5 and "...take captive every thought, bringing it (your thoughts) to the obedience of Christ."

Prophecy: I prophesy over you that the enemy's power over your life is broken and the negative thoughts you have taken as truth are stripped from you this day, and you are free!

Today's affirmation: I come into full agreement with God's thoughts concerning myself and my life. I am who God says I am, I can have what He says I can have, and I can do what He says I can do! I am royalty and I am living an overcoming, victorious life!

Prayer: Lord, I thank you for revealing the truth that I can control my thoughts. Thank you, Jesus, for helping me think on the things that are good, lovely and that keep my life moving in the direction that glorifies you, in Jesus' name.

Reflections

Day 9

Under the Influence

Today's insight: My real enemies are not people, but Satan who uses people.

Today's verse: Ephesians 6:12-13 (KJV)

"For we wrestle not against flesh and blood, but against principalities, against powers, against the rulers of the darkness of this world, against spiritual wickedness in high places. Wherefore take unto you the whole armor of God, that ye may be able to withstand in the evil day, and having done all, to stand."

We have all heard the phrase "under the influence." It often means that someone has been exposed to an outside substance that has altered their behavior in some way. That outside substance can be some type of drug, alcohol, or mind and mood-altering substance. Without realizing it, we have all been affected by someone who's been under the influence. But we tend to wrongly accuse the person rather than identifying the real influencer, Satan and the fallen angels (demons) who are actually using the person as a host!

You see, Satan and all demons are disembodied spirits. In order to get their job done to steal, kill, abuse, destroy, lie, control, cheat, bond and oppress, they need a physical body. They are willing to use anyone who, through ignorance, generational and familial curses, or on purpose will allow them to express themselves. But the good news is that the blood of Jesus Christ can set anyone free and release them from the influence of the enemy of our souls.

So, instead of getting angry with that person who's wronged you, get angry and exercise your authority as a believer over the real enemy. You've been given authority to bind and loose (Matt. 18:18), have been commanded to love your enemies and pray for those who persecute you, and show you are a child of your Heavenly Father! (Matt. 5:44,45) Begin to see, not with just your physical eyes but spiritual eyes, and recognize those who are really under the influence.

Prophecy: I prophesy over you this day that your spiritual eyes are being opened and you will now begin to see in a realm of the spirit that you have never seen before. (2 Kings 6:17)

Today's affirmation: I am in Christ Jesus and seated together with Him in heavenly places, which is a place of authority to exercise dominion over every one of my enemies. (Ephesians 2:6)

Prayer: Thank you, Lord, for showing me how to love people who are being used by the enemy and recognize the real enemy. I receive victory in this area, in Jesus' name.

Reflections

Day 10

Willing to Change

Today's insight: I must be willing to do things God's way rather than my own!

Today's verse: Isaiah 1:19 (AMPC)

"If you are willing and obedient, you shall eat the good of the land;"

Have you ever been determined that you are going to do things your way, regardless of what outside or inside wisdom and counsel you have received? We all have, and I can tell you from experience, sometimes that's not the wisest thing to do. You see, we as born-again, spirit-filled believers have a guide on the inside of us. He is the person of the Holy Spirit, and it is His job to lead and direct our lives to a place of peace, joy, and victory. (Romans 8:14)

The problem is sometimes we don't always follow His leading, but, in our own stubbornness, we're convinced we know better. Because we reason from our natural thinking or we're simply not willing to obey the person of the Holy Spirit, we think our way is better, or it's too difficult to do what He's asking us to do. Here is a wisdom key. If you and I are ever going to walk in and experience God's best blessings, we had better structure our lives around Jesus and only do what He heard the Father say to do; it will lead us from one victory to another.

The story of Jonah is a great example of not wanting to obey God because of personal preferences. After three days in the belly of a whale, Jonah quickly learned it's better to obey the first time than live in chaos and darkness. Decide today that you will be willing and obedient to all God says to you!

Prophecy: I prophesy this day that sensitivity to the voice of the Holy Spirit is released, and you will hear His voice more accurately than you have ever heard before.

Today's affirmation: I am obedient to God, so I eat the good of the land. I am enjoying God's best blessings in my life and family.

Prayer: Thank you, Lord, for helping me live in a place of obedience to your written and spoken word, in Jesus' name.

Reflections

Day 11

Supernatural Increase

Today's insight: God is not limited to the natural!

Today's verse: Genesis 26:12 (AMPC)

"Then Isaac sowed seed in that land and received in the same year a hundred times as much as he had planted, and the Lord favored him with blessings."

I love how God breaks all natural laws in order to bless His children! In today's text, we read how Isaac, the son of Abraham the patriarch, was in Egypt in the midst of a famine. When there was no water, no food, and no provision (or at least extremely limited provision), God told him to do something that, in the natural, made no sense.

He told him to plant his crops. In obedience, he plants crops and at harvest time, not only did Abraham receive a crop, but God added His supernatural presence on the seeds that were planted. The harvest was one hundred times the size of what was originally expected! You see, no matter how small or limited your financial seed may be, plant it into the rich soil of God's kingdom. He has the ability to cause supernatural multiplication, even in the midst of what the world calls an economic recession.

Prophecy: I prophesy that today is the day of divine turnaround in your economy, and you have stepped into a season of one hundred times as much as you sow into the Kingdom of God!

Today's affirmation: My days of lack, debt and recession are over. The Lord is increasing me more and more, me and my children!

Prayer: Thank you, Lord, for allowing me to live the life of abundance you have destined for me so I can always live a life of active generosity, in Jesus' name.

Reflections

Day 12

Satan's Top Ten Playlist!

Today's insight: Recognize strife and confusion, two of Satan's top 10!

Today's verse: Genesis 13:7-8 (ASV)

"And there was a strife between the herdsmen of Abram's cattle and the herdsmen of Lot's cattle: and the Canaanite and the Perizzite dwelt then in the land. And Abram said unto Lot, Let there be no strife, I pray thee, between me and thee, and between my herdsmen and thy herdsmen; for we are brethren."

If you're a music lover like myself, then you probably have a favorite genre of music on your smartphone, laptop or computer. Among those songs, you probably have a list of top ten favorites. Did you know that Satan has a top ten list as well? Not of music, but of tricks, wiles and schemes he likes to use to gain access into the lives of people, especially believers!

In today's passage, we see how Abraham recognized the plot of Satan to get him into strife and cut off the blessing. Abraham put a stop to it immediately by separating from his nephew Lot. Strife will short-circuit the blessing of God in your life quicker than anything else! We're given deeper insight in the New Testament that where there is strife and confusion, there is a doorway leading to every evil work (sickness, poverty, confusion, division and destruction)! Learn to guard your heart by refusing to enter into strife with anyone, including your spouse, friends, family, coworkers and anyone else the enemy may be using to gain access to your life and take you into custody at his will (2 Timothy 2: 24-26).

If you have allowed yourself to be handcuffed and taken into custody through strife by Satan, then repent; ask for and receive forgiveness so that you may go free and enjoy the blessings of God unhindered by the enemy.

Prophecy: I prophesy to you this day that your spiritual eyes are now open, and you will immediately recognize and cut off strife's access to your life.

Today's affirmation: I decree that I live free from strife, and I walk and live continuously in the love of God!

Prayer: Thank you, Lord, for always helping me to walk in love toward others and never be in strife or contention, in Jesus' name.

Reflections

Day 13

Am I Really Spiritually Mature?

Today's insight: My spiritual growth will be determined by how teachable I remain!

Today's verse: Proverbs 1:7 (NIV)

"The fear of the Lord is the beginning of knowledge, but fools despise wisdom and instruction."

Have you ever been corrected? How did you receive it? Did you go away upset and angry, or did you go away thanking God and the person He used to bring correction to you, be it a friend, your spouse, pastor, boss, parents, family or a complete stranger? In today's passage, we are challenged to do a self-assessment of how well we do when we are corrected; we are placed in either one category or another, wise or foolish! If we are wise, we receive the correction, make the changes we need to make, and continue to develop in our spiritual growth.

If we are foolish, we get angry, upset, and many times, break fellowship with the person God has used to correct us. You see, our flesh doesn't like to be corrected and as a result, we have a bunch of spiritually-immature believers who get angry with their spiritual leaders and bounce around from one failure to another, never maturing. God wants to release your rightful kingdom inheritance, but He only releases it to the spiritually-mature.

In the kingdom, the more mature you are, the more resources and responsibilities you can be entrusted to handle (faithful over little, ruler over much). We all think we're more mature than we are, but it's our Father God who determines when we've reached spiritual maturity (Galatians 4:1- 2).

The next time you're being corrected, ask yourself: What does God's word say about this? Do I need to change? Be determined to pass the test so you can receive the promotion and promises you have been waiting and praying for. And thank God, He loves you enough to correct you! (Proverbs 9:8-9).

Prophecy: I prophesy this day that your spirit is open to receive correction, no matter who it comes through!

Today's affirmation: I am aligning my life with the Word and spirit of God daily, and therefore I receive correction and am growing up spiritually so that I may receive my full inheritance.

Prayer: Thank you, Lord, for loving me enough to correct me through your Word and others you have placed in my life to correct me, in Jesus' name.

Reflections

Day 14

The Commanded Blessing

Today's insight: Proper posture and position is required. Am I positioned for the blessing?

Today's verse: Psalms 133:1,3 (KJV)

"Behold, how good and how pleasant it is for brethren to dwell together in unity! As the dew of Hermon, and as the dew that descended upon the mountains of Zion: for there the Lord commanded the blessing, even life forevermore."

Did you know that God wants to command the blessing on you? What's the blessing? I'm glad you asked! The blessing is an invisible force that surrounds you and empowers you to succeed, grants you supernatural favor, makes your name famous and distinguished, and allows you to be generous and affect the world for good (Genesis 12:2 AMP). It allows you to provide solutions for any problem on any level that's presented on the planet, be it physical, mental, spiritual, social, natural or financial. Wow! That's a powerful force!

One of the major spiritual keys for walking in this commanded blessing is unity among fellow brothers and sisters. This is why Satan fights unity on every level-between family, friends, business partners, churches, marriages, companies and any other relationships where people are in partnership with one another!

Our target scripture today gives us powerful insight into experiencing the commanded blessing on our lives! It's simple but can be challenging to "fight for unity." So, the next time you're tempted to be the source of contention, ask yourself, "Do I really want to disqualify myself from the commanded blessing?"

Prophecy: I prophesy to you this day that there is a release of the spirit of unity in your life. You are stepping into a season of being a catalyst for unity in your sphere of influence!

Today's affirmation: I strive to dwell together in unity in all my relationships and as a result, I receive the commanded blessing that impacts lives globally.

Prayer: Lord, I thank you that you have conferred the blessing on my life. I will always protect it by walking in love according to your word, in Jesus' name.

Reflections

Day 15

God, Is That You?

Today's insight: I can personally learn to consistently hear the voice of God.

Today's verse: John 10:27 (NIV)

"My sheep listen to my voice; I know them, and they follow me."

As a born-again believer, did you know that you can hear the voice of God for yourself? Many believers would rather hear God through a famous preacher or the latest prophet. Although God does use spiritual leaders to speak to us, He desires to speak to us personally. Imagine if you were a parent and you only communicated with your kids through someone else. You would miss out on having a more meaningful, loving, and personal relationship with them.

In today's passage, we see that God does speak to us personally, the question is – do we recognize His voice? Whatever He says to you will always be in perfect alignment with scripture. In other words, He will never tell you to do something that violates or contradicts the Bible. No matter where I travel in the world, the minute I phone my kids and they hear my voice, they recognize it's me because of the quality time I have spent with them their entire lives. They know they are going to receive direction, encouraging words, answers to questions they have and always "I love you!" Our Heavenly Father is the same way. Tune in today and listen for the voice of the one who loves you and me most.

Prophecy: I prophesy this day that your spiritual ears are being opened now. You will hear and recognize the voice of God like never before!

Today's affirmation: I am a child of a God who has an ear to hear His voice accurately, and I follow Him in complete obedience! (John 10:27)

Prayer: I thank you, Lord, that I call and you answer me. I hear your voice clearly and am always led by your spirit, in Jesus' name.

Reflections

Day 16

Supernatural Wisdom!

Today's insight: I am not limited to what I've learned through formal education!

Today's verse: 1 Kings 3:12 (AMPC)

"Behold, I have done as you asked. I have given you a wise, discerning mind, so that no one before you was your equal, nor shall any arise after you equal to you."

Did you know that you're not limited to what you've learned in institutions of learning? That is if you are born again. You see, you have the Godhead living on inside you, and according to what God has to say about you: *"But of him are ye in Christ Jesus, who of God is made unto us wisdom, and righteousness, and sanctification, and redemption."* – 1 Corinthians 1:30 (KJV).

Wow! You have the person of wisdom, Jesus, living inside you! That means you can never encounter a problem or situation you can't get out of! If there is a way out, you can access wisdom to get you out – wisdom for the board room, bedroom, university, classroom or operating room. Wherever you need answers, just listen on the inside and expect the Holy Spirit to release wisdom and reveal your exit strategy!

King Solomon was given wisdom that caused him to excel above everyone else. It prospered him, caused him to be sought out to judge hard matters, and affected the entire kingdom over which he reigned! Scripture tells us that Jesus, a wisdom greater than Solomon, is here and living on inside every born again believer. Will you let wisdom flow out of you to affect the realm to which you have been called to influence and govern?

Prophecy: I prophesy this day that the circumstances and situations that cause you to be stuck are dissolving because of the new release of the wisdom of God flowing out of you!

Today's affirmation: I have the wisdom of God living on the inside of me!

Prayer: Thank you, Lord, for the revelation that I have eternal wisdom living on the inside of me. I release my faith to access and operate in this wisdom daily, in Jesus' name.

Reflections

Day 17

A Complete Recovery

Today's insight: No matter what I've lost, God wants to restore it!

Today's verse: 1 Samuel 30:18-19 (KJV)

"And David recovered all that the Amalekites had carried away: and David rescued his two wives. And there was nothing lacking to them, neither small nor great, neither sons nor daughters, neither spoil nor anything that they had taken to them: David recovered all."

In life, all of us have experienced loss in one way or another, perhaps a job, business, friend or relationship. You may have suffered the loss of a contract, peace, a marriage, a home, your confidence, health or happiness. I want you to know that God has plans to restore everything and every area in your life where you've experienced loss! In the passage for today, King David, upon returning from war, discovered a reality of complete loss: his family, home and the entire city had been attacked, raided and torched to the ground. Everything and everyone was gone, including his family! The enemy (Satan) loves to raid, plunder and torch our lives (John 10:10).

You may be experiencing great loss today. Like David, your situation may seem impossible to recover from, but God is a master in restoration! Matthew 19:26 declares, *"But with God, all things are possible."* All that He requires is faith in him! As you read and meditate on today's devotional, God is speaking to you and reminding you that no matter what the enemy has stolen from you, God has plans to restore it all. After crying his eyes out until there were no more tears, David gathered his emotions and inquired of God. He asked, *"Should I pursue the enemy?"* God answers David with an affirmative, *"Yes! Pursue the enemy, for you shall surely overtake them, and without fail recover all!"* (I Samuel 30:8)

Prophecy: I prophesy to you that this is your day of restoration and recovery of everything in your life that the enemy has stolen! You will lack nothing! Only good shall come to you.

Today's affirmation: God is behind the scenes working in my life to restore everything that has been stolen. I am recovering all! (Psalms 138:8, Philippians 1:6)

Prayer: Thank you, Lord, for restoring everything in my life that I have lost. You delight in showing mercy and I receive full restitution, in Jesus' name.

Reflections

Day 18

The Privilege of Generosity!

Today's insight: The happiest people in life are those who spend their lives giving to and unselfishly serving others

Today's verse: Luke 6:38 (NIV)

"Give and you will receive. Your gift will return to you in full – pressed down, shaken together to make room for more, running over, and poured into your lap. The amount you give will determine the amount you receive."

What is generosity? Defined in the dictionary, it is the quality of being kind and generous. Generosity in real time is about giving more than what's required. It's about giving our time, talents, and treasure to benefit and bless others without strings attached or ulterior motives.

Jesus gives us the secret to being truly joyful and determining the size of harvests in our own lives. He lived out generosity and modeled it for everyone who followed Him. As Christ followers, we are called to do the same in our generation.

Our church family in Miami, Florida, collectively gave more than two million dollars to our community in 2022. Those generous donations were given to individuals, organizations, and churches throughout Miami and the United States to continue to impact and transform lives, some of which were impacted by devastating hurricanes. This same generosity helped to educate and train pastors, feed families during Thanksgiving and place a smile on the faces of hundreds of kids during Christmas who would have otherwise gone without presents.

The generosity of our church fed the homeless, impacted those who are incarcerated, canceled debt for many and paid off student loans for others. Ministers were sent to the mission field, the gospel was preached on all social media platforms, causing thousands to be encouraged and swept into the Kingdom of God, all because of the generosity of thousands of people in a local assembly who have the revelation that generosity is our privilege. It is not surprising that this offering at the end of the year, right before Christmas, was the largest the ministry had ever received at one time. What triggered that offering was the spiritual principle that Jesus taught:
"It is more blessed to give than to receive." (Acts 20:35)

The secret to experiencing true happiness and real joy that is not based upon your outward circumstances is to be generous with your time, talents and resources. It will make you among the happiest people on earth.

Prophecy: I prophesy that the lavish God is lavishing His abundance on you from this day forward.

Today's affirmation: Because of God's love and goodness to me, I am committed to being generous to others every day of my life.

Prayer: Thank you, Lord, for the privilege to be generous, because you're always generous to me, in Jesus' name.

Reflections

Day 19

Seven Years of Plenty

Today's insight: Recognizing seasons of abundance is paramount to being properly sustained during times of famine.

Today's verse: Genesis 41:29,30

"The next seven years will be a period of great prosperity throughout the land of Egypt. But afterward, there will be seven years of famine so great that all the prosperity will be forgotten in Egypt."

One of the greatest insights we can gain from the story of Joseph is that we learn to store up during times of abundance, because seasons in life can change abruptly, leaving the abundant seasons all but forgotten.

"... time and chance happen to them all." – Ecclesiastes 9:11

No matter your background, race, color, position in life, social or economic status, everyone reading this book has experienced a time when things were moving at warp speed and in the right direction. Then suddenly life happened! You hit a proverbial "pothole." You lost the job, faced divorce, received the diagnosis, a loved one died, the business failed, your contract was suddenly terminated, that promising relationship you thought would last forever ended, a global pandemic arose, the life savings was lost in the investment that promised to make millions…

In every one of the above scenarios, there was a time when life seemed perfect, and all of a sudden everything went in the opposite direction. You see, no matter how great life is, real life circumstances occur. It's not a matter of if, but rather when. The most important thing we can learn from the story of Joseph – who God used to sustain all of Egypt and the region around him during a global famine – was to prepare during times of abundance. Store up reserves! Joseph received wisdom to store up "twenty percent" of everything harvested during the seven years of plenty.

Times of abundance can represent many things. Financial abundance, physical health, quality relationships, spiritual capacity and more. All of which have the potential to change, and if you have managed well during those times of abundance and stored up properly, you will make it through those tough times, minimizing the damage.

Prophecy: I prophesy over you this day that you will not miss your hour of visitation but will discern your seasons of abundance.

Today's affirmation: I am determined to live life intentionally, storing up reserves for every area of my life.

Prayer: Lord, thank you for the seasons of abundance. Help me to steward them well and bring glory to you in every season of my life, in Jesus' name.

Reflections

Day 20

Why Am I Facing This Challenge?

Today's insight: Don't accept the label of your challenge but dare to believe who God has called you to be – a winner!

Today's verse: Judges 6:12-13 (NIV)

"When the angel of the Lord appeared to Gideon, he said, "The Lord is with you, mighty warrior." "Pardon me, my Lord," Gideon replied, "but if the Lord is with us, why has all this happened to us? Where are all his wonders that our ancestors told us about when they said, 'Did not the Lord bring us up out of Egypt?' But now the Lord has abandoned us and given us into the hand of Midian."

Life's challenging times can leave you feeling so deflated that enjoying victories can appear to be a far-fetched dream or wishful thinking! In today's verse, we read the story of Gideon and the Israelites (belonging to God), who were being severely persecuted by their enemies, the Midianites and Amalekites. They were constantly being harassed and having all their food supply completely destroyed, leaving them with nothing to eat and greatly impoverished. During this difficult time for Israel, Gideon received an unexpected and very surprising visit from an angel.

The angel greeted him and immediately announced, "The Lord is with you" and then addressed him as a "mighty warrior." He then revealed how heaven planned to use him to deliver his nation. Because of

Israel's current situation, Gideon had already concluded that God had abandoned His people, which he sarcastically shares at the appearance of the Angel of the Lord. Nothing could be further from the truth! God promises to never leave or forsake us. And like Gideon, we must also have faith to believe that God is faithful.

Just like He delivered the Israelites and used Gideon to lead the battle, He has empowered us with the Holy Spirit who will cause us to win every battle and lead us into our own personal victories, no matter how bleak our current situation and circumstances might be.

Prophecy: I prophesy to you this day that the battle is the Lord's and the victory is yours.

Today's affirmation: My challenges don't define me – God does!

Today's prayer: Lord, always allow me to live with a spirit of faith instead of doubt and unbelief, especially during challenging and difficult times, in Jesus' name.

Reflections

Day 21

Back-to-Back Blessings!

Today's insight: God's blessing on your life will increase exponentially!

Today's verse: Amos 9:13-15 (MSG)

"Yes indeed, it won't be long now," God's decree. "Things are going to happen so fast your head will swim, one thing fast on the heels of the other. You won't be able to keep up. Everything will be happening at once—and everywhere you look, blessings! Blessings like wine pouring off the mountains and hills. I'll make everything right again for my people Israel: "They'll rebuild their ruined cities. They'll plant vineyards and drink good wine. They'll work their gardens and eat fresh vegetables. And I'll plant them, plant them on their own land. They'll never again be uprooted from the land I've given them." GOD, your God, says so.

Can you handle the blessing of God? I pray that you can because according to today's verse, when God releases His blessing upon your life, everything will happen so fast, you literally won't be able to keep up. You will begin to experience back-to-back blessings! That means everything you touch will begin to work: your family, ministry, business, relationships and finances!

The blessing is God's supernatural empowerment upon your life, an invisible heavenly shield that guarantees success, protection and unusual results in your life. It caused Isaac to prosper in the middle of a famine,

David to defeat Goliath, Daniel to be protected in a den of lions, and Joseph to go from the pit to the palace without a resume. When you're made aware that you've received the blessing, life will take on an entirely new meaning.

You will know it is impossible for you to fail in life. You will truly begin to live out Daniel 11:32, *"The people who know their God shall be strong and do exploits."* Today, lean in to this powerful benefit your Heavenly Father has lavished upon us.

Prophecy: I prophesy to you today that back-to-back blessings overtake your life.

Today's affirmation: I wear the blessing and it cannot be removed or reversed!

Prayer: Thank you, Lord, for bestowing upon me the divine empowerment to win in all areas of my life. I am blessed and a blessing to others, in Jesus' name.

Reflections

Day 22

Enduring the Test of Time

Today's insight: In consistency lies the power – Gloria Copeland

Today's verse: Hebrews 13:8 (NIV)

"Jesus Christ is the same yesterday and today and forever."

One of the greatest truths we can use to strengthen our faith, especially during times of adversity, is that God never changes. He is always good, His mercy endures forever and He is consistently consistent. He is the same yesterday, today and forever. That means He is still doing exactly what He did when he walked on planet Earth.

He is still healing hearts and minds, bringing freedom to those wearing chains of bondage and sharing the good news that there is a new government called the Kingdom of God, and once you become a citizen through faith in Him, the benefits are out of this world (Psalms 103).

He forgives our sins, heals our disease, delivers our life from destruction, crowns us with loving kindness, and fills our life with good things, just to name a few.

The next time you're tempted to believe that God has changed with the times, stop and remind yourself that He never changes (Malachi 3:6).

Prophecy: I prophesy that the unchanging God is moving constantly in your life to bring radical change.

Today's affirmation: God is consistently good to me and He never changes.

Today's prayer: Father, in the name of Jesus, help me to always remember that you love me unconditionally and that you have been, you are presently, and you will always be good to me because you never change.

Reflections

Day 23

Right on Schedule

Today's insight: God will bless me on schedule.

Today's verse: Deuteronomy 28:11,12 (MSG)

"GOD will lavish you with good things: children from your womb, offspring from your animals, and crops from your land, the land that GOD promised your ancestors that he would give you. GOD will throw open the doors of his sky vaults and pour rain on your land on schedule and bless the work you take in hand. You will lend to many nations but you yourself won't have to take out a loan."

Have you ever struggled with waiting for God's promises to show up in your life? If we are really honest, I think we all have. We somehow believe that we know the best time for God to show up. When we don't see immediate changes or answers to our prayers, we often become anxious and somehow think that God has forgotten us.

Today's verse is a great reminder that God will bless us on schedule. He knows the best timing to manifest why we're believing in Him. Mary and Martha, friends of Jesus, accused Him of arriving too late to heal their brother Lazarus, who was very ill. Jesus had delayed His coming by four days and as a result of his delay, Lazarus died.

When Jesus arrived, He quickly proved He's never too late. He raised Lazarus from the dead and demanded that he be released from the grave clothing his body had been wrapped in (John 11). He presented him alive right on schedule! Trust God that He will bless you on schedule. (Philippians 4:6)

Learn to trust God's timing for your life, knowing that He loves you and knows what's best.

Prophecy: I prophesy that the God of the breakthrough is breaking through for you this very day.

Today's affirmation: I'm encouraged daily that God knows the best timing to manifest His promises in my life.

Prayer: Lord, forgive me for the times I have been anxious and impatient waiting for you to come through. Help me to always believe that you're behind the scenes working on my behalf. I trust you with every detail of my life (Prov 3:5-7), in Jesus' name.

Reflections

Day 24

Completely Outdone

Today's insight: God is exceeding my every expectation!

Today's verse: Ephesians 3:20 (TPT)

"Never doubt God's mighty power to work in you and accomplish all this. He will achieve infinitely more than your greatest request, your most unbelievable dream, and exceed your wildest imagination [a] He will outdo them all, for His miraculous power constantly energizes you."

Has God ever exceeded your expectations? I love today's verse because it is a reminder that God wants to outdo my request! In other words, He wants to exceed my current expectations. One translation of this passage states that He wants to do exceedingly, abundantly, above all you and I could ask, think, imagine, hope for, pray or dream. That's wonderful news, especially if you're anything like me. I have a pretty tall imagination and can dream some pretty wild dreams!

When we, His children, begin to receive the revelation that our Father is omnipresent, omniscient and has every resource at His disposal – be it spiritual, physical or yet to exist – and begin to expand our thinking and realize that He wants to partner with us on earth to do great things that testify of His greatness, we will be outdone with his acts toward us. God loves to lavish His kids with goodness! He proved it by feeding an estimated 20,000 people with two fish and five loaves, just a little boy's lunch.

After everyone ate, there were still twelve baskets left over for the little boy to take home. Talk about a return on his investment! Jesus caused Peter, a commercial fisherman, to catch a year's supply in one day, so much so that he had to call for others in the fishing industry to come and help gather the great catch of fish.

Prophecy: I prophesy that multiplied increase is entering into your hands today.

Today's affirmation: Today, and every day of my life, I'm expecting God to exceed all my expectations!

Prayer: Thank you, Lord, for shattering every glass ceiling in my life – whether perceived or real – and taking me to the top, making me the standard, in Jesus' name.

Reflections

Day 25

The Satisfied Life

Today's insight: God wants me to live a satisfied life.

Today's verse: Psalms 90:14 (NLT)

"Satisfy us each morning with your unfailing love, so we may sing for joy to the end of our lives."

Are you living a satisfied life? One that's content and full of joy? Or are you living an unfulfilled life that's full of fear, stress and anxiety? If you are, I have good news for you today: God wants to satisfy you each morning with His unfailing love. Why? I'm glad you asked! He wants all His children to experience His unconditional love and be full of joy until the very end of our lives.

Happiness is based upon outward circumstances, but joy, which is a fruit of the spirit (Galatians 5:22), is inherent to our born-again spirit. When joy is properly developed, we learn to live independent of our circumstances and have a continuous song in our hearts and a skip in our step, displaying for all the world to see and know that our God reigns over all the earth.

Lean into this verse today and every day of your earthly existence and begin to command your morning! Let the world see firsthand that our life in Christ is a satisfied life regardless of our circumstances.

Prophecy: I prophesy over you that from this day forward, only good shall come to you!

Today's affirmation: Because of my life in Christ, I'm living a satisfied life!

Prayer: Satisfy me early, Lord, that I might sing for joy for the rest of my life. Thank you, Lord, for helping me to live a life of contentment, being balanced so as not to settle for less than your best for my life, in Jesus' name.

Reflections

Day 26

Your Benefits Package!

Today's insight: My new life in Christ entitles me to Kingdom benefits!

Today's verse: Psalms 103:2 (KJV)

"Bless the Lord, O my soul, and forget not all his benefits."

Have you ever had the experience of beginning a new career or becoming employed by a new company? If so, you are quite familiar with being required to attend that company's orientation sessions. During this process, one of the things they inform you of is the benefits you are entitled to for becoming an employee.

Benefits such as life and health insurance, vacation and paid time off, retirement programs and potentially company shares. Because of your new employment, you are now able to receive these benefits. Today's devotion is an important part of your orientation in the Kingdom of God.

"Who forgives all your sins and heals all your diseases, who redeems your life from the pit and crowns you with love and compassion, who satisfies your desires with good things so that your youth is renewed like the eagle's." – Psalm 103:3-5 (NIV)

These are just a few of the benefits we should remind ourselves of daily! The best part is, unlike most earthly companies' policies, there is no waiting period; you can receive these rewards the minute you are born again and begin your new life in Christ!

Go ahead and take advantage of your new Kingdom benefits of forgiveness of sin, healing from sickness and disease, protection, unconditional love and renewed strength.

Prophecy: I prophesy this day that the revelation of Kingdom benefits is flooding your spirit, causing breakthroughs in your life like never before!

Today's affirmation: I am a Kingdom citizen with Kingdom benefits that I access daily.

Prayer: Thank you, Lord, for my Kingdom benefits! I receive them today, in Jesus' name.

Reflections

Day 27

Freedom from Containment

Today's insight: As a Christ follower, the only limit in your life is the one that's in your mind; no one can stop you but you!

Today's verse: Exodus 8:27-28 (NIV)

"We must take a three-day journey into the wilderness to offer sacrifices to the Lord our God, as he commands us." Pharaoh said, "I will let you go to offer sacrifices to the Lord your God in the wilderness, but you must not go very far. Now, pray for me."

Do you ever feel like you are being contained or limited in life? Like there is an invisible chain around your feet, feeling like the elephant at the circus chained to a stake limiting how far he can go? Maybe it's with your finances, career or business, relationships or even in ministry. If so, it might be that you're encountering the same demonic spirit we read about in today's verse that controlled Pharaoh.

God had used Moses and Aaron, his brother, to give very specific orders to *"let His people go,"* but Pharaoh, in his hard-heartedness and stubbornness, had refused to allow the Israelites who had been enslaved for 430 years to leave Egypt – at least until he experienced a series of plagues orchestrated by God through Moses. During one of the afflictions, the plague of flies, there were swarms of flies throughout Pharaoh's palace, the houses of his officials and throughout the land of Egypt, except for Goshen where the Israelites lived. This plague could have ended immediately at Moses' request to God, but only if Pharaoh released the Israelites. Ten different times Moses petitioned that the Israelites be allowed to go into the wilderness and make sacrifices to God, but Pharaoh, in his desire to control and compromise with Moses, replied *"I will let you go to offer the sacrifices to the Lord, but you must not go very far."*

The enemy of Christ, Satan himself, loves to try and contain us in life, telling us that we can only go so far. We can rent or lease but not own our own home or multiple properties. We can work for minimum wages, but not be entrepreneurs and thriving business owners. We can earn the high school diploma, but never earn the doctorate degree. We can own and operate one business, but not have multiple businesses or ministry campuses. You see, at one time or another we have all been victims of Satan's lies that tried to convince us that we can only go so far. But today, as the light of God's word enters your heart, I announce to you as a Christ follower and by the power of the Holy Spirit that you will break and exceed every limitation Satan has set on you.

Prophecy: I prophesy over you that every limitation on your life is now shattered.

Today's affirmation: I will exceed every limitation that the devil and his agents have placed on me.

Prayer: Lord, thank you for breaking every barrier in my life and causing me to enter the destiny you have prepared for me, in Jesus' name.

Reflections

Day 28

The Real Secret to Success

Today's insight: It will be evident that God is with me because His presence guarantees my success.

Today's verse: I Samuel 18:14

"David continued to succeed in everything he did, for the Lord was with him."

One of the most important truths you can begin to perceive is that if you are a follower of Jesus Christ, He is with you. When you invite Him to be involved in your everyday affairs, He will guarantee your success. His presence makes the difference! Often we make our plans and ask God to sign off on them rather than first seeking God for His plans for our life, the ones He already blessed. You see, God is very much interested in you prospering in every area of your life (3 John 1:2, Psalms 35:27). David is such a wonderful example of this.

From his time as a shepherd, defeating Goliath, and running from Saul for his very life, to him being crowned King over all of Israel, David's testimony and heart's cry was, *"Please don't ever banish me from your presence or take your Holy Spirit away from me."* (Psalms 51:11)

David knew the secret to winning in life was the presence of God in his life.
If you are reading or listening to this devotion today, do as David did and cry out for the presence of God to

always accompany you everywhere you go and in everything you do. You will be guaranteed success.

Prophecy: I prophesy that because the Lord is with me, wherever I go, only good shall come to me.

Today's affirmation: I meditate on God's word night and day; therefore, I am prosperous and have good success. (Joshua 1:8)

Prayer: Lord, I thank you for your exceeding, great, and precious promise to always be with me. I am confident that because you are with me, I will always win, in Jesus' name. (2 Corinthians 2:14)

Reflections

Day 29

The Most Important Relationship

Today's insight: Spending quality time with God will enhance every area of your life.

Today's verse: Job 22:21 (NKJV)

"Now acquaint yourself with Him, and be at peace; thereby good will come to you."

Do you currently have friends or acquaintances who only contact you when they are in need? Truth be told, we can all think of that person or, unfortunately, we have been that person.

Today's passage gives us some very valuable insight into our most important and valuable relationship: our relationship with God. Out of anyone you can befriend, the friend who will stick closer than any brother is Jesus. As we mature and develop in life, sometimes the people we thought would be in our lives for a lifetime leave us for various reasons.

Like rocket boosters, there are times as we ascend in life – spiritually, mentally, emotionally, even financially – people drop off. But the one friend who will never leave or forsake us is Jesus, and the better we get to know Him by spending quality time with Him in prayer, scripture, worship, reflection, the better our life becomes.

If you desire to live in the peace that surpasses all understanding and see the goodness of God show up in your life daily, then make time with Him your priority! There is not a more valuable relationship.

Prophecy: I prophesy that you are encountering the presence of God in a fresh way from this day forward.

Today's affirmation: My time with Jesus is my highest priority!

Prayer: Lord, thank you for the privilege to get to know you personally and intimately. I am forever grateful for your love for me. I love you because you first loved me, in Jesus' name I pray.

Reflections

Day 30

Putting Blame in Its Proper Place

Today's insight: Lacking revelation can lead to misplaced blame.

Today's verse: Job 1:22 (NIV)

"In all this, Job did not sin by charging God with wrongdoing."

Have you ever been blamed for something you didn't do? I have and know how frustrating it can be. I was once stopped by a police officer on a routine traffic stop. He informed me that my license had been suspended for failure to pay several citations in various cities where I personally had not been. I proceeded to tell him that it must be an error because I had not visited any of those cities. Needless to say, I spent the next several weeks attending court, gathering the citations that were in question, and defending myself before traffic judges in order to clear my name and have my license reinstated. I had been falsely accused and was made to deal with the consequences.

In today's verse, we gain valuable insight into the character of Job, a man who loved God passionately and who was targeted by Satan. The attack of the devil on his life because of his love for God and spotless character caused him to suffer unbearable loss. He lost his good health, his family, his thriving businesses, his wealth and even lifelong friends turned against him! Everyone around him concluded that he must have done something wrong and God was punishing him. In reality, that was not the case. It was Satan's hatred of him and attempt to get him to curse God and die (a suggestion made by his wife). Instead, Job did something that would solidify his future victory and restoration. Without full insight, he refused to blame God for the tragedy in his life.

He simply trusted God for the unanswered questions and believed that this terrible season would pass. It did, and in the end, God restored to Job twice as much as he had lost. Double for his trouble! The next time you're tempted to blame God for tragedy in your life, refuse! Put the blame in the right place, on the thief who comes to steal, kill and destroy. (John 10:10)

Prophecy: I prophesy over your life today that for your shame and disappointment, you shall receive double.

Today's affirmation: The Lord is always good and all that's good and perfect comes from Him. (James 1)

Prayer: Thank you, Lord, for the revelation that you are always good and only desire the best for me. I'm eternally grateful for your love, which you constantly display toward me. Forgive me for the times I've blamed you for the bad things that have happened in my life; I see now that you are perfect in all your ways, in Jesus' name I pray.

Reflections

Day 31

Willing to Leave the Status Quo!

Today's insight: "Mediocrity will always be offended by excellence" - Dr. Marina McLean

Today's verse: Genesis 12:1-2 (NIV)

"The Lord had said to Abram, "Go from your country, your people, and your father's household to the land I will show you. I will make you into a great nation, and I will bless you; I will make your name great, and you will be a blessing."

Mediocre: Of only moderate quality, not very good.

As you read the definition of the word mediocre, were you automatically forced into doing a self-assessment? Did you ask yourself, *Is my life, family, business, ministry, marriage, health, relationships, and spiritual life of only moderate quality? Is my life very good?*

Whether you realize it or not, you and I are called to live an excellent life. Many times, we have reduced all or some parts of our lives to simply settling for where we are, rather than striving for the place of greatness and the good life that God wants us to live. I can hear the doubt coming against your mind even now as you read and listen. *You mean to tell me God wants me to have a good life?* Yes, He does! Let me prove it to you.

"For we are God's [own] handiwork (His workmanship), recreated in Christ Jesus, [born anew] that we may do those good works which God predestined (planned beforehand) for us [taking paths which He prepared ahead of time], that we should

walk in them [living the good life which He prearranged and made ready for us to live]." – Ephesians 2:10

This is one of my favorite passages in the entire Bible because it's a promise that God not only wants me to have a good life, but that he's already made provisions and arrangements for me to have that good life! That promise alone shatters the mindset of a mediocre, second-rate, living-beneath-the-privileged life!

When you start to meditate on that promise, you can only imagine what kind of resources the King of the Universe has at his disposal. He says in one passage, "My God shall supply all of your needs according to his riches in glory by Christ Jesus!" Philippians 4:19

Wow! His riches are in glory! That is a revelation! It means that God is not limited to the resources on the planet but, as He's proven before, has the ability to release heavenly substance to meet our needs. *When has He done this before?* In Exodus 16 we see God release manna (heavenly vanilla wafers, as I like to call it) to feed the children of Israel in the wilderness.

This was a manifestation of the Glory of God! He has also released rain in times of drought, downloads of wisdom, strategy, creative ideas, and spiritual gifts. All of these were manifestations of the glory of God, and since He is the same yesterday, today and forever, only Heaven knows what awaits us!

Prophecy: I prophesy you will no longer live in mediocrity.

Today's affirmation: My life in Christ is one that's designed to model excellence!

Prayer: Lord, please help me to live in the reality of my new identity in Christ, knowing that you have created me for more.

Reflections

Reflections

Reflections

Made in the USA
Columbia, SC
03 November 2024